LIFE ON A HORSE FARM

LIFE ON A HORSE FARM

by Judy Wolfman
photographs by David Lorenz Winston

Carolrhoda Books, Inc. / Minneapolis

To Gwen, Dennis, Sarah, and Daniel Mills, our sincere thanks for sharing your knowledge about horses, your time, and your beautiful farm.

—J.W. and D.L.W.

Carolrhoda Books, Inc.
A division of Lerner Publishing Group
241 First Avenue North
Minneapolis, MN 55401 U.S.A.

Website address: www.lernerbooks.com

LIBRARY OF CONGRESS CATALOGING-IN-PUBLICATION DATA

Wolfman, Judy.
    Life on a horse farm / by Judy Wolfman ; photographs by David Lorenz Winston.
       p.   cm. — (Life on a farm)
    Includes index.
    ISBN 1-57505-517-1 (lib. bdg. : alk. paper)
  1. Race horses—Juvenile literature. 2. Horse farms—Juvenile literature.
3. Farm life—Juvenile literature. I. Winston, David Lorenz, ill. II. Title. III. Series.
SF302 .W66 2002
636.1'2—dc21   00-011044

Manufactured in the United States of America
1 2 3 4 5 6 – JR – 07 06 05 04 03 02

CONTENTS

At **Home**
with
HORSES

Living on a horse farm is an amazing way to grow up. Few people have a chance to ride a horse or even touch one. But I've been around horses all my life. My name is Sarah Mills, and I live on a horse farm called Willow Tree Farm. My dad grew up here. He learned about raising racehorses from his father. When Pap retired, Dad took over.

An acre is almost as big as a football field, so our 110-acre farm covers a lot of land.

Pap heads out to the field to mow.

Our farm is truly a family business. Pap still works here, even though Dad runs the farm. Mom has a job off the farm, working for a veterinarian. But she also helps Dad with his work. My brother, Daniel, does tough jobs like mending fences and growing the hay we feed to the horses. I'm too young to handle a horse alone, but I can do some chores on the farm.

About twenty-five horses live on our farm. We own a few of them. But most belong to Dad's clients. People who want to raise racehorses bring their **mares** to stay here. (A mare is a female horse.) Our **stallion**, or male horse, **breeds** the mares to make them pregnant. Dad's clients pay him to raise and train the mare's **foal**, or baby. But the foal belongs to its mother's owner, not to us.

8

Daniel and I try not to get too attached to the mares and foals because we know they won't stay on the farm forever. But we always do anyway!

We've had Mikey for five years. Horse owners send mares for him to breed from as far away as North Carolina.

Our stallion's name is Like a Brother, but we call him Mikey. He's a type of horse called a Thoroughbred. Thoroughbreds are faster than most other horses and can run long distances. That's why they're used for racing. Mikey's dad won a famous horse race called the Kentucky Derby, so Mikey has a good background. That's what people look for in a stallion.

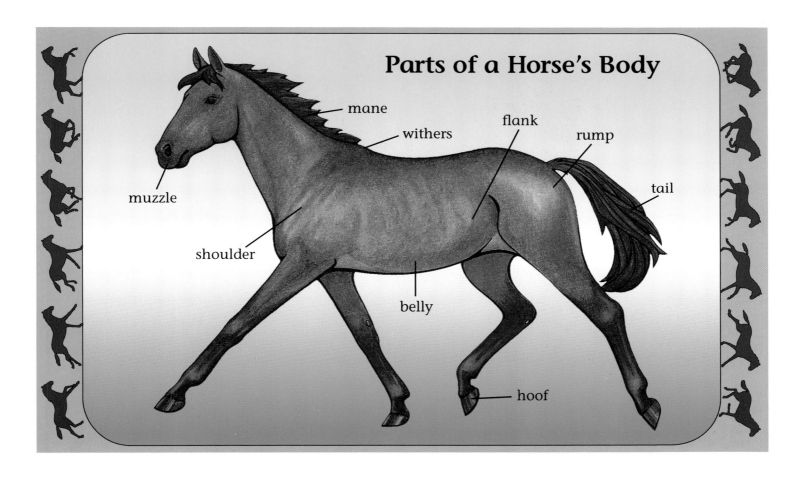

Parts of a Horse's Body

mane

flank

rump

withers

muzzle

tail

shoulder

belly

hoof

The time of year that Mikey breeds a mare is important. Horses race against others of the same age, starting around age two. No matter when a Thoroughbred foal is born, its first birthday is January 1 of the next year. Even if a foal is born in December, it still becomes "one year old" on the next January 1. (Then it's called a **yearling**.) So horse owners want their foals to be born as early in the year as possible. That way, they'll have more time to grow and train before they race. Dad keeps this in mind as he decides when Mikey should breed a mare.

'When we see a mare spread her legs and squat, we know that she's ready to be bred.

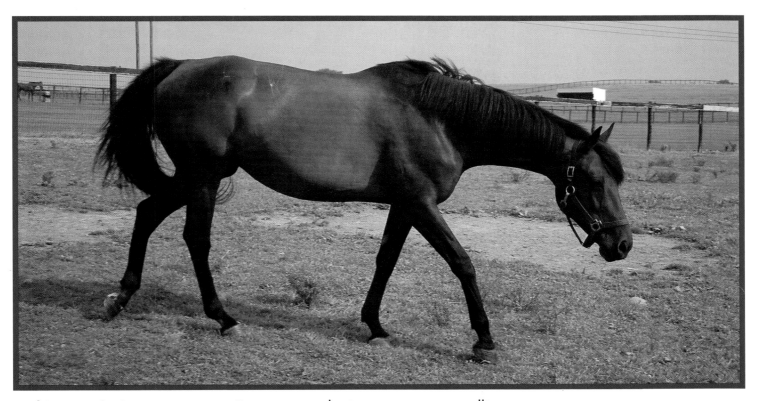

This mare isn't pregnant yet. Some mares don't get pregnant at all, so we have to return them to their owners.

We know a mare is ready to be bred when she starts acting silly. If she blinks a lot, arches her tail, and squats down to pee just a little bit, she's in **heat.** That means she's able to become pregnant. Dad puts the mare in a stall in the barn. Then he brings Mikey in.

The two horses check each other out. If the mare doesn't like Mikey, she'll lay her ears back along her neck and make ugly faces. She hollers and might even try to attack him. Then we have to take Mikey out. But if the mare likes him, Dad lets them both out of the stall. Mikey breeds the mare out in one of our **paddocks,** or fenced pastures.

The vet is checking to see if this mare is pregnant. The machine on the floor will tell us if we can expect a new foal next year.

Twenty days later, a veterinarian visits. The vet does an ultrasound to see if the mare is pregnant. This test shows a picture of the inside of the mare's body on a small TV screen. If we see a small black dot, we know the mare is pregnant.

The foal will be born about eleven months and ten days after the mare was bred. Some mares may have the baby earlier and some later. But usually they're right on time.

When a mare is close to foaling, it's important to keep her nearby. We put her in a paddock close to the barn during the day and in a stall in the barn at night.

When a mare is ready to foal, or give birth, her tummy is huge. Her **udder,** or milk bag, swells, and her **teats,** or nipples, get waxy. She may begin to drip her milk. Mares don't like to be watched during their foaling. They often give birth at night. But Dad needs to see each birth in case the mare needs help. So he puts a special girth, or strap, around the mare. The girth has sensors that go off when the mare lies down to give birth. Then an alarm rings in my parents' bedroom, and they know it's time.

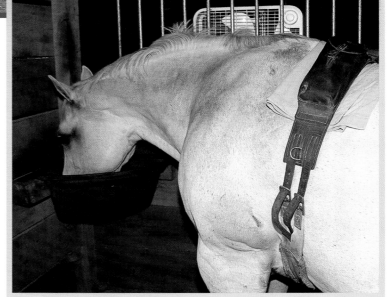

This mare is wearing an alarm so that Mom and Dad will know when she's ready to give birth.

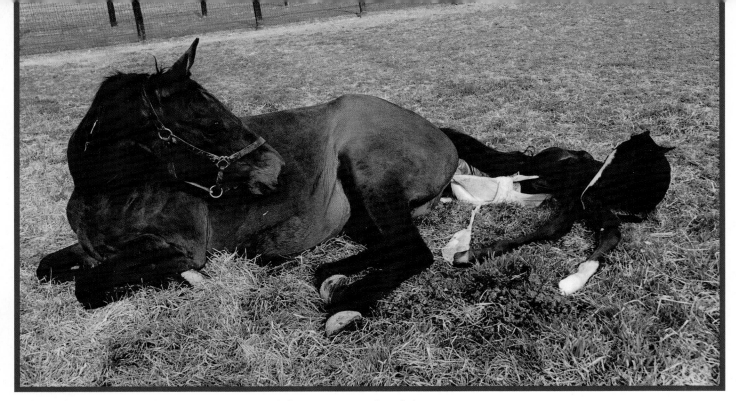

This foal was just born. You can see the sac on its back legs. The umbilical cord is still attached to its belly.

Once I saw a birth. When the mare squeezed her muscles, a thin, filmy bubble came out of her back end. This was the sac, a thin layer of tissue that surrounds the foal. I could see the foal's head and front legs through the sac. The mare kept pushing. With each push, I saw more of the foal. Then it was all out! The sac broke.

The foal's **umbilical cord** broke, too. This cord is like a lifeline. While the foal grows inside its mother, it gets food and oxygen through the cord.

The foal began breathing air for the first time and opened its eyes. It was all wet and looked cold. Dad and I could see that it was a **filly,** or female foal. (A male foal is called a **colt.**)

This little foal is tired after a difficult birth. A healthy foal weighs about 100 pounds and is about 3 feet tall. It's close to the size of a Labrador retriever, but it's taller and has longer legs.

The filly rested while her mother licked her clean. The mare nickered to the filly and gently nudged her, trying to get her to stand up. The filly stuck out her front legs and tried to stand. But her legs were wobbly and got all tangled up. The filly fell down, rested a bit, and tried again—over and over. Finally, she stayed up. Then she found the milk bag under her mother's tummy. She **nursed**, or sucked milk from the teats, for a long time.

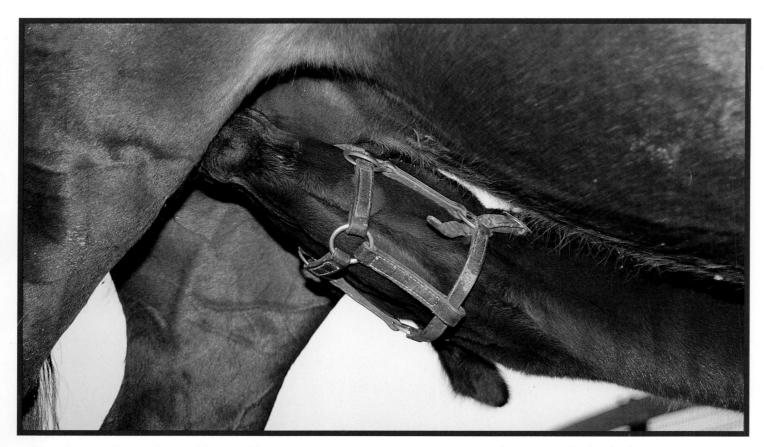

This foal is three days old. Dad has started to train it to wear a set of straps called a halter.

A colt takes its first wobbly steps.

We're always happy when a foal is born without trouble. But sometimes a mare needs help. One mare had a very large foal, and Dad had to help pull it out. Some foals are turned upside down inside the mare. Dad has to turn them around before they can come out. Sometimes a foal's sac doesn't break. Dad has to cut the sac so the foal can take its first breath. I'm proud of my dad—he's saved the lives of a lot of foals.

Mares whinny and snort to communicate with their foals.
This foal is listening for its mother's voice.

Getting to know a new foal is one of my favorite things about living on a horse farm.

A mare should be at least three years old when she has her first foal. She can be bred again about ten days after the baby is born. But every so often, the mare is given a year off to rest before she has another foal. There's no rest for us, though—we need to keep working every single day.

No HORSING Around

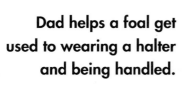
Dad helps a foal get used to wearing a halter and being handled.

A new foal begins to train for life as a racehorse when it's just two or three days old. Dad puts a set of straps called a **halter** on the foal's head. When he lets the foal into or out of the barn, he attaches a rope to the halter. Then he walks gently with the foal. This is how it learns what it's like to be led.

When the foal is two weeks old, Dad puts a light saddle on it. A week later, he puts a **bridle** on the foal, too. Like a halter, a bridle fits over a horse's head. But it also has a metal part called a **bit** that fits into the horse's mouth.

The bridle and bit allow a rider to guide and control the horse. The foal isn't big enough to be ridden yet. But it needs to get used to having something in its mouth. So it wears the bridle and bit for an hour or so each day.

Before the foal can be trained to wear a bridle, it must learn to be led by a rope.

This mother and foal have their own paddock where the mother can care for her foal.

For the first two or three weeks, we keep the foal and its mother by themselves in a paddock. There they have lots of room to run and plenty of fresh grass to eat. At first, the foal just nibbles and plays with the grass. After about three weeks, it seems to enjoy eating it. Then we put the foal and mare in a paddock with other mothers and babies. The foal nurses, eats grass, runs, and plays with its new friends.

Two new friends run in a paddock.

Another change comes when the foal is about six months old. We **wean** it, or take it away from its mother so it will stop nursing. This is not a happy time for the foal. We put it in a paddock. The mother is put in a separate paddock, as far away as possible.

A young foal looks for its mother during weaning.

This mare is happy to have some peace and quiet after taking care of her foal for so long.

The foal runs up and down the field. It neighs and makes a lot of noise, trying to call its mother. Sometimes the mare answers. But usually she doesn't seem to pay attention. By this time, most mares are happy to just eat grass and not have to worry about nursing a baby!

Daniel puts out feed for a mare. Later, she enjoys a drink of fresh water.

Most of the time there's more than one weaned foal in a paddock. The foals keep each other company. Instead of nursing, they eat grass and hay. They also eat the grain mixture we give them. This mixture contains bran, molasses, vitamins, and minerals. In time, the foals get used to not having their moms around.

Along with food, the horses need water. There's an automatic water fountain in each paddock and each stall in the barn, so the horses can drink anytime.

When it's cold or rainy, the horses go into the shelter in their paddock. They stand close to each other to keep warm. But if the weather gets too bad, we bring them into the barn.

Horses can get sick or hurt easily, so we have to keep an eye on them. Dad and I walk through the paddocks often. Dad checks the horses for wounds or sores. He looks at their eyes, legs, and hooves. I help him make sure there's plenty of food, water, and hay. A horse has a small stomach, so it doesn't eat a lot of food at one time. Instead, it nibbles throughout the day. So it's important to make sure that a horse always has enough hay to eat.

Dad also takes care of the horses' teeth. Horses have flat teeth, so they can't chew food the way people do. They just grind it. The grinding wears down the teeth and makes some of their edges sharp. The sharp edges could cut the horse's tongue or cheek. To protect the horse, Dad files down the edges every so often.

This mare likes having her coat shampooed. I wear a special rubber glove that helps make the coat clean and shiny.

Sweeping the barn isn't much fun, but it's one of my most important jobs.

Since our horses stay in the paddocks, they get their baths from Mother Nature when it rains. But if it's hot and dry, we hose the horses down. Then we shampoo them and dry them off. Next we brush and comb them. Sometimes I braid their manes, but that takes too long to do very often.

I also help by mucking out, or cleaning, the barn. I sweep out the stalls, put down sawdust for the horses' bedding, and add fresh hay. I check the water in the automatic fountains to make sure it's clean. If the fountains are dirty, I scrub them. It's hard work, but it's good to know I'm helping our horses.

A horse's hooves grow faster in the summer, so Dad has to trim them more often.

Dad and I take care of the horses' hooves every few weeks. Dad holds up each hoof, one at a time. I hand him his hoof tools. First, he scrapes the dirt out of the hoof's ridges. Then he carefully trims the hoof with a hoof knife. (This is done because a horse's hooves grow like a person's fingernails do.) I watch Dad carefully because someday I hope to do these chores, too.

32

All this time, the fillies and colts keep growing. When a colt is nine months old, a veterinarian comes to the farm to **geld** it. The vet gives the colt some medicine to relax it. Then the colt gets a shot to make it fall asleep. While the colt sleeps, the vet does an operation to remove the colt's testicles. (Testicles are male body parts that are important for breeding.)

After this operation, the colt is called a **gelding.** Geldings keep their mind on their work and don't go around looking for a filly to breed. They'll make good racehorses someday. The fillies will, too. But first, they all have a lot more to learn!

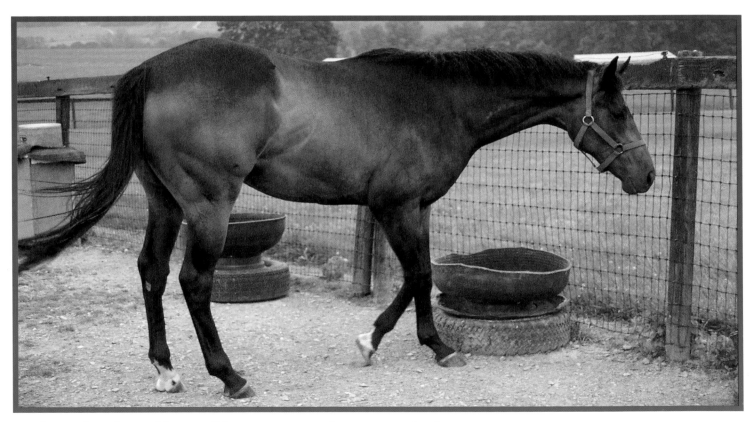

We hope that this gelding will be a great racehorse someday!

Training for the TRACK

After a foal becomes a yearling, its training gets more serious. When the yearling is used to being handled, we hook it to our indoor walking machine to make sure it gets plenty of exercise. The horse walks about fifteen minutes every day for six weeks.

Next, we let the yearling rest in the paddock for six months. Then Mom or Dad puts a bridle on the horse again. This time, straps called **reins** are attached to the bridle. Dad walks behind the horse, steering it. After a couple of days, the horse knows which way to move.

Mom carefully puts a bridle on a horse. The horse isn't very used to the bridle, so it's a struggle.

Wisdom of Solomon, a horse that Dad trained, is in the lead!

It takes about two years for Dad to train a horse. Then the horse goes back to its owner or to the racetrack. A new trainer teaches the horse to carry a rider. It learns to gallop and race. When the horse can gallop fast and far, it's ready for its first official race.

We keep a couple of our own racehorses at the track. Dad takes care of them, but he doesn't ride them in races. He hires a professional rider called a **jockey**. One of our horses raced off and on for ten years. That's a long time—most horses race only about five years. His name was B. A. Captain, and he won lots of races.

Dad and I are proud of Wisdom of Solomon and the jockey who rode him.
Like this one, most jockeys are small, so they aren't too heavy on the horse's back.

This is my first pony, Peaches. I've outgrown her, so we had to give her away. But I still visit her whenever I can.

I wouldn't want to be a jockey myself, but I like to ride. I took my first riding lesson a few years ago on a pony named Patches. (A pony is a type of horse that grows to only a small size.) I found out that I needed a lot more training—just like a foal! Patches headed straight toward a jump, and I got scared. I ended up falling off the pony. I scraped my elbow really badly and didn't want to get back on. It took me a long time to get over being afraid. But after a while, I got a pony of my own named Peaches.

Since then, I've started taking lessons again. I go twice a week to a nearby farm. I've graduated from a pony to Surprise, a small horse that my teacher owns. After lots of practice, I've learned to mount, walk, and trot pretty well. I have my own riding helmet and saddle, too.

Mom helps me with my riding outfit.

The saddle is very heavy.

I check to make sure the saddle is secure before I ride.

A full-grown horse is a big animal. A Thoroughbred weighs about 1,000 to 1,400 pounds. People measure a horse's height in units called hands. One hand is 4 inches. An adult Thoroughbred stands about 15 to 17 hands high from the ground to the highest point of the withers (the ridge between the horse's shoulder bones). That's at least 60 inches, or 5 feet high—a lot taller than I am! I can remove Surprise's bridle myself, but I need a stepstool to put on the saddle. I'm still growing, so I should be able to do more as I get bigger.

Sitting tall on a horse is the best feeling in the world!

I'm always careful when I get off Surprise—it would be a long way to fall!

Here we are after another great ride.

Surprise waits patiently while I remove her bridle.

I don't think I'll ever stop loving horses. I'd like to be a veterinarian someday. But it would also be great to have a few horses to take care of and ride. Then, if I ever get married and have children, they would have horses to love, too. Who knows? Maybe I'll live on a horse farm for the rest of my life. I wouldn't mind that one bit!

Fun Facts about HORSES

Horses have very good memories. A horse will remember a special experience—good or bad—for many years.

Thoroughbred horses were first bred in England. The first Thoroughbred brought to North America was a stallion called Bulle Rock who crossed the ocean to Virginia in 1730.

A horse whisperer is a person who is said to be able to communicate with horses in their own language.

What's the only land animal with eyes that are larger than a horse's?
THE OSTRICH!

Watch out if you see a horse with its ears laid back against its head. It's probably getting ready to kick!

When a foal is born, its legs are almost as long as an adult horse's! The rest of the foal's body catches up to the legs as the foal grows.

A horse's **wide nostrils** help it take in lots of air as it runs.

A Thoroughbred horse can run a mile in about 1.5 minutes!

Learn More about HORSES

Websites

Horse Country
<http://www.horse-country.com>
Horse fans can play games, try out recipes for horse treats, and meet other horse-loving kids here. If you're looking for a pen pal, try this site—be sure to read the e-mail safety page first!

International Museum of the Horse
<http://www.imh.org/imh/imhmain.html>
Check out this information-packed site for online exhibits about horse history, horse art, and dozens of different horse breeds.

Nature: *"Horses"*
<http://www.pbs.org/wnet/nature/horses/index.html>
This public television website offers an illustrated history of horses and their life with humans.

Books

Henderson, Carolyn. *Horse and Pony Breeds.* New York: DK Publishing, 1999. Get the fast facts about different types of horses and ponies in this easy-to-read guide.

Hill, Cherry. *Your Pony, Your Horse: A Kid's Guide to Care and Enjoyment.* Williamstown, MA: Storey Communications, 1995. Do you have a horse of your own or a chance to take riding lessons? Check out this friendly guide—written especially for kids—to choosing, understanding, and caring for horses and ponies.

Patent, Dorothy Hinshaw. *Horses.* Minneapolis: Lerner Publications Company, 2001. How do wild horses live and grow? Find out in this colorful, photo-filled book.

Rodenas, Paula. *The Random House Book of Horses and Horsemanship.* New York: Random House, 1997. This detail-packed volume offers an introduction to horse breeds, training, and activities such as 4-H and riding clubs.

GLOSSARY

bit: a metal piece that fits into a horse's mouth to hold a bridle in place

breeds: makes pregnant

bridle: a type of headgear that is used to control a horse's movement

colt: a young male horse

filly: a young female horse

foal: a young horse

geld: to remove body parts that allow a male horse to breed

gelding: a male horse that cannot breed

halter: a set of straps that fit over a horse's head so that the horse can be led

heat: the time when a female horse can become pregnant

jockey: a person who is paid to ride a horse in a race

mares: female horses

nursed: drank milk from a mother's body

paddocks: fenced pastures

reins: straps that are attached to a bridle to guide a horse

stallion: a male horse that can breed

teats: small, raised parts on a female horse's belly. A baby horse drinks milk through its mother's teats. (Teats are also called nipples.)

udder: the part of a female horse that makes milk. Teats are located on the udder.

ultrasound: a test that a veterinarian performs to find out if a female horse is pregnant

umbilical cord: the lifeline that connects a mother and baby while the baby grows inside the mother

wean: to separate a young animal from its mother so that it will stop nursing

yearling: a year-old horse

INDEX

About the AUTHOR

Judy Wolfman is a writer and professional storyteller who presents workshops on creativity and storytelling. She also enjoys both acting and writing for the theater. Her published works include children's plays, numerous magazine articles, and Carolrhoda's Life on a Farm series. A retired schoolteacher, she has two sons, a daughter, and four granddaughters. She lives in York, Pennsylvania.

About the PHOTOGRAPHER

David Lorenz Winston is an award-winning photographer whose work has been published by *National Geographic World,* UNICEF, and the National Wildlife Federation. In addition to his work on the Life on a Farm series, Mr. Winston has been photographing pigs, cows, and other animals for many years. He lives in southeastern Pennsylvania. To learn more about Mr. Winston's work, visit his website at <http://www.davidlorenzwinston.com>.